Oceans
and Seas

KINGFISHER
LONDON & NEW YORK

Copyright © 2004 by Kingfisher
Published in the United States by Kingfisher,
175 Fifth Ave., New York, NY 10010
Kingfisher is an imprint of Macmillan Children's Books, London.
All rights reserved.

First published in hardcover as *Kingfisher Young Knowledge: Oceans and Seas* in 2004
First published in this format in 2007

Distributed in the U.S. by Macmillan, 175 Fifth Ave., New York, NY 10010
Distributed in Canada by H.B. Fenn and Company Ltd.,
34 Nixon Road, Bolton, Ontario L7E 1W2

Library of Congress Cataloging-in-Publication Data has been applied for.

ISBN: 978-0-7534-6165-5

Kingfisher books are available for special promotions and premiums.
For details contact: Special Markets Department,
Macmillan, 175 Fifth Avenue, New York, NY 10010.

For more information, please visit www.kingfisherpublications.com

Printed in China
5 7 9 8 6 4
4TR/0110/WKT/RNB(RNB)/140MA/C

Acknowledgments
The publishers would like to thank the following for permission to reproduce their material. Every care has been taken
to trace copyright holders. However, if there have been unintentional omissions or failure to trace copyright holders,
we apologize and will, if informed, endeavor to make corrections in any future edition.
b = bottom, *c* = center, *l* = left, *t* = top, *r* = right

Photographs: *cover t* Getty Images (Getty); *cover b* Natural History Picture Agency; 1 Getty; 2–3 Getty; 4–5 Corbis; 6 Getty; 7*tr* National
Geographic Image Collection (NGIC); 7*cl* Nature Picture Library; 7*br* Minden Pictures/Frank Lane Picture Agency; 8–9 Corbis; 9*tl* Alamy;
9*b* Corbis; 11*b* Corbis; 12–13 Getty; 13*tl* Oxford Scientific Films (OSF); 13*cl* OSF; 13*br* Corbis; 14 Press Association, London; 15 Corbis;
15*t* Corbis; 16–17 Getty; 16*b* Science Photo Library (SPL); 17*t* OSF; 18–19 Ardea; 19*tl* NGIC; 19*br* Ardea; 20 Getty; 21 Getty; 21*b* Nature
Picture Library 22–23 Corbis; 22*bl* Corbis; 23*tl* Getty; 24–25 NGIC; 26*bl* Nature Picture Library; 27*tl* Nature Picture Library; 27*cr* Nature
Picture Library; 27*b* Nature Picture Library; 28–29 Corbis; 28*bl* Getty; 30*b* Getty; 31 Ardea; 31*bl* Ardea; 32*bl* Corbis; 33*t* Minden
Pictures/Frank Lane Picture Agency; 33*b* Image Quest 3D; 34–35 Getty; 34*bl* Image Quest 3D; 35*tl* Nature Picture Library; 36–37 Corbis;
36*bl* SPL; 37*tr* SPL; 38 Corbis; 39 Getty; 40*bl* Getty; 40–41 Getty; 41*t* Getty; 48 Minden Pictures/Frank Lane Picture Agency.

Commissioned photography on pages 42–47 by Andy Crawford.
Project maker and photo shoot coordinator: Miranda Kennedy.
Thank you to models Lewis Manu and Rebecca Roper.

SCIENCE KIDS

Oceans and Seas

Nicola Davies

KINGFISHER
NEW YORK

Contents

Planet ocean

Only one third of Earth is dry land, so our planet looks blue when seen from space. The rest of the planet is made of water, and there is life in every ocean and sea!

An ocean is a large sea

Sunlit surface

The ocean's surface is full of tiny plants and animals called plankton, which bigger creatures, such as these jellyfish, eat.

Staying hidden

Many animals, like this octopus, prefer the deeper water of the middle ocean. There they can hide from predators and be safe from storms.

Deep and dark

The deepest waters are completely dark and cold. Food is hard to find, so animals there have big mouths— and eat anything!

predators—animals that hunt and eat other animals

Salty seas

All seas and oceans are salty, with around 1.2 ounces of salt in every 35 ounces of water. That is as salty as one large spoonful of salt in half a bucket of water!

Saltiest sea

The Dead Sea in Asia is so salty that when its water is turned into vapor by the Sun, the salt that is left behind is hard, white lumps.

vapor—*a mist or gas given off when something is heated*

Salty sources

Volcanic hot spots on land and on the seabed add salt to seawater when they release hot gases and molten rock. Rivers wash salt from the land into the seas and oceans.

Grains of salt

Some of the salt we put on our food comes from the sea. Sea salt is broken up into small pieces so that we can sprinkle it on our food.

volcanic—from a volcano or area where molten rock or steam comes to the surface

Underwater landscape

Hidden below the sea is a world of high mountains, wide plains, and deep valleys—an entire landscape as interesting and varied as the one on dry land!

Flattest and deepest

Almost half of the deep seabed is a very flat abyssal plain. Even deeper are the ocean trenches, which plunge more than 32,000 feet below the surface.

abyssal plain—a large, flat area of land on the seabed

Mountaintop islands

When volcanoes form on the seabed, they grow into mountains. These can get so tall that they stick out of the sea and form islands.

Black smokers

Deep seawater is usually very cold, but at volcanic spots called black smokers water three times hotter than boiling water gushes through cracks in the seabed.

trenches—long, narrow valleys that are usually formed next to islands or mountains

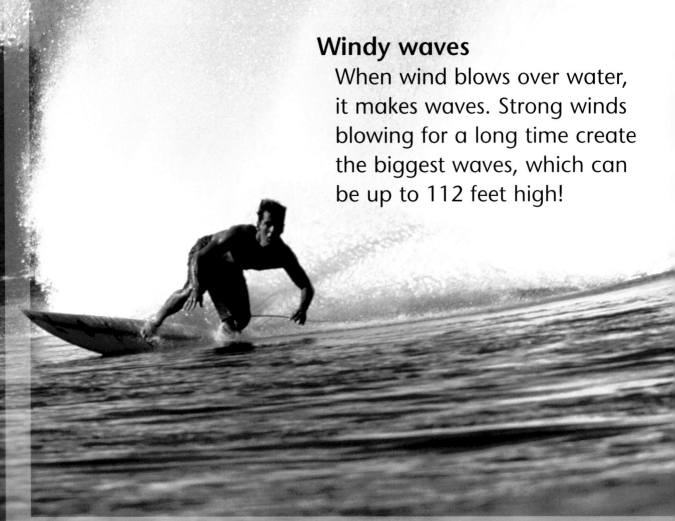

12) Tides and waves

Seawater is always moving. It is stimulated by the heat of the Sun and the cold of the ice at the North and South poles, pushed by winds, and pulled by the Sun and the movement of the Moon.

Windy waves

When wind blows over water, it makes waves. Strong winds blowing for a long time create the biggest waves, which can be up to 112 feet high!

coasts—*shores, places where seas or oceans and land meet*

Tide out, tide in

The Moon pulls water toward it as it travels around Earth, causing the seas and oceans to move away from the coasts. This movement causes tides. Most tides happen twice each day—the sea moves away from the shore (tide out) and then back again (tide in).

tide out

tide in

Eating away land

In some places waves wash away beaches and cliffs, changing the shape of the coastline in just a few days.

Weather-making sea

The oceans create weather by warming or cooling the air over them, forming wind and clouds. Ocean currents carry warm and cold weather around the planet.

Hooray for rain!
Clouds from the Indian Ocean bring heavy rains to Asia and Africa. Without the rains, crops would not grow.

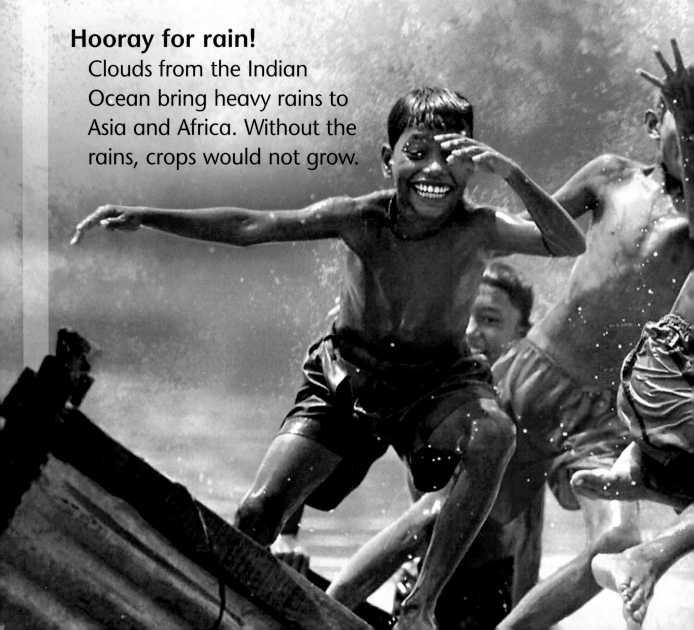

Hurricane!

Warm, tropical seas sometimes heat the air above them so much that they cause wind and rain to build into a giant spinning storm, or hurricane. This type of huge storm can destroy whole towns.

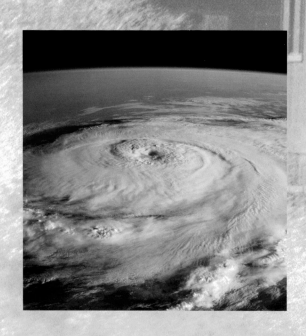

El Niño

Every few years a strange warm current called El Niño sweeps along the west coast of South America, causing extreme weather across the world—devastating storms, droughts, and even heavy snow.

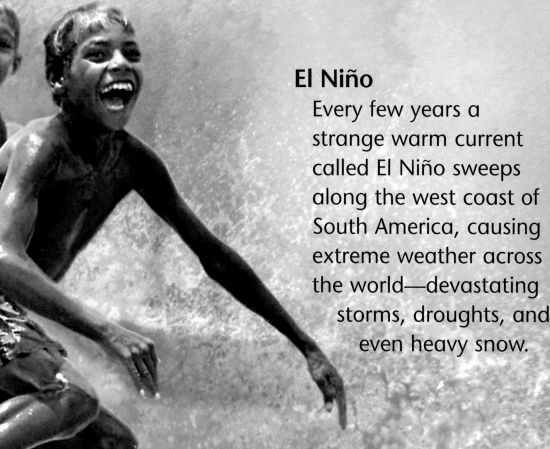

currents—rivers of seawater flowing inside a sea or ocean

Living history

Life on Earth began in the sea, billions of years before there was life on land. Some of these early life-forms are alive in the sea today!

First life on Earth?
Stromatolites are layers of millions of tiny creatures. They look just like stromatolites that lived three billion years ago.

Living fossils
The coelacanth fish was known only by fossils that were millions of years old— until living coelacanths were discovered in 1938.

fossils—the remains of ancient animals or plants that have turned into rock

Unchanged habits

Every year horseshoe crabs surface from deep water to lay their eggs on sandy beaches, just like they have done for 400 million years!

billion—*1,000 million years, written like this: 1,000,000,000*

Fish rule

There are more than 20,000 different types of fish in all shapes and sizes, and most of them live in the oceans and seas.

Ocean hunters

Big fish, such as this blue shark, are the predators of the sea. Most sharks hunt animals to eat and swim very fast so that they can catch their food.

Fish or seaweed?

The leafy sea dragon looks so much like seaweed that it can hide among the plants and not be seen by other fish that might want to eat it.

Safety in numbers

In a school of fish there is a greater chance of spotting danger (many eyes), as well as a smaller chance of being eaten (many other fish could be eaten instead)!

school—*a large group of one type of fish*

Ocean mammals

Sea mammals are shaped for swimming. They have smooth, streamlined bodies that can slide through the water, and they can hold their breath for a long time when they dive.

Sea fliers

Sea lions use their webbed front feet like oars to row them along— fast! It is like underwater flying, and it makes catching fish easy!

streamlined—having a smooth body shape that moves easily through water

Legless dolphins

Dolphins do not have back legs at all! They swim by beating their tails up and down and steer with paddle-shaped feet called flippers.

Underwater herbivores

Dugongs also use their tails and flippers for swimming. These large, heavy animals graze on plants called sea grasses, so their other name is "sea cow."

herbivores—*plant-eating animals*

Super seabirds

Seabirds are tough! They fly hundreds or thousands of miles every year to find food at sea. They survive storms and rough seas, and they still find their way back to land to nest. Phew!

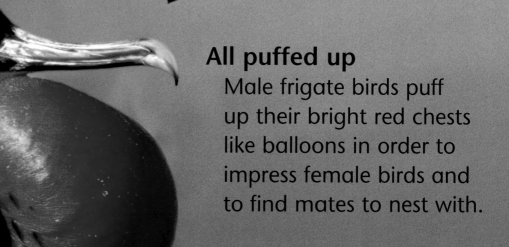

All puffed up

Male frigate birds puff up their bright red chests like balloons in order to impress female birds and to find mates to nest with.

Tiny traveler

The tiny arctic tern travels almost 15,000 miles every year, from the Arctic Ocean to the Antarctic Ocean and then back again.

Long wings

Huge wingspans of up to 11.5 feet carry albatross over the stormiest oceans in search of food.

Diving for dinner

Puffins dive for food, using their wings underwater like paddles. They catch small fish to feed to their chicks on land.

wingspans—*distances between wing tips*

Who eats whom?

Ocean life, just like life on land, depends on plants. Plants are eaten by herbivores, and herbivores are eaten by carnivores— this is called a food chain.

Big mouth, short chain!
The whale shark is the world's biggest fish (up to 50 feet long)! Its food chain is very short because it feeds on the smallest animals and plants in the sea—plankton.

carnivores—animals that eat meat

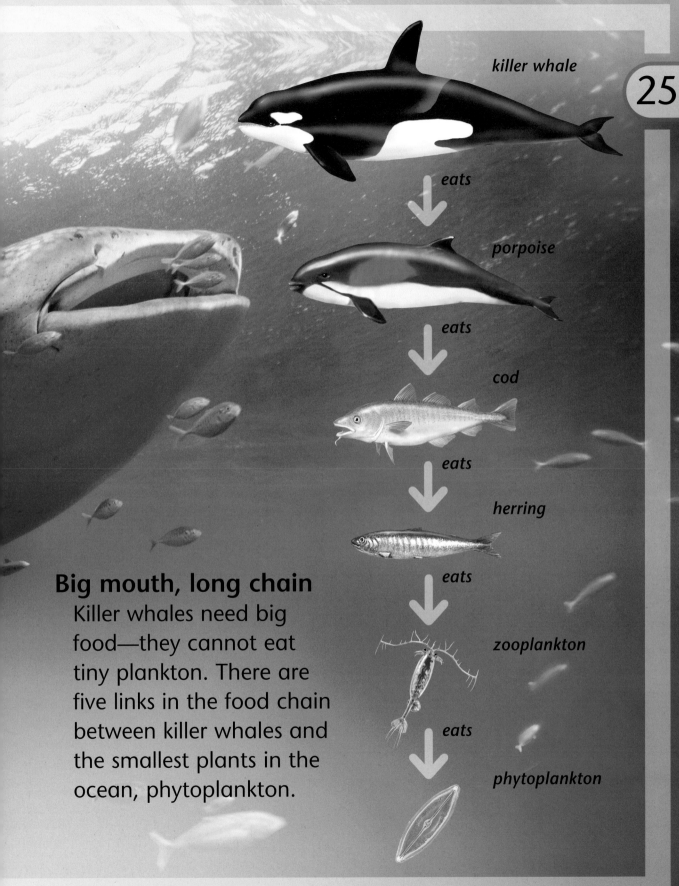

killer whale

eats

porpoise

eats

cod

eats

herring

eats

zooplankton

eats

phytoplankton

Big mouth, long chain

Killer whales need big
food—they cannot eat
tiny plankton. There are
five links in the food chain
between killer whales and
the smallest plants in the
ocean, phytoplankton.

zooplankton—*a type of plankton that is an animal, not a plant*

Coral reefs

In tropical seas, where the water is warm and clear, corals grow like forests of small pink, yellow, and white trees. They are full of colorful fish and many other life-forms.

Clever clowns!

Little clown fish can hide from danger among the stinging tentacles of big anenomes since anenomes never sting their own clown fish!

Super slug
The sea slug's bright colors are a warning to predators that its orange skin is poisonous!

Plantlike corals
Corals look like plants, but they are really animals with soft bodies that are protected by hard, stony skeletons. They are related to anenomes.

tentacles—long, flexible parts of an animal, used for gripping, feeling, or moving

Kelp jungles

All over the world, where the sea is cool and the coastline is rocky, there are underwater jungles of huge seaweed called kelp.

Jungle eaters . . .
Sea urchins eat kelp, and, although they are small, they can munch their way through a forest of seaweed.

. . . and jungle savers

Luckily, many animals eat sea urchins.
Seals, dogfish, lobsters, and sea otters,
such as this one floating in a kelp forest
off the west coast of the U.S., love to
snack on the spiky animals.

Frozen feasts

Antarctica is the huge frozen land around the South Pole. It looks like an icy desert, but the ocean around it is full of fish, birds, seals, and whales.

Penguin crowds

Seven types of penguins live in the Antarctic, but these Adélies are the most common. There can be five million of them in one nesting area!

schools—groups of whales

Whale schools

Humpback whales, as well as 14 other types of whales and dolphins, travel to the Antarctic every summer just to feed.

. . . and here is what they eat . . .

Krill! These shrimplike animals are not big—only 1.5 inches long—but there are many of them. One swarm can cover 45,000 football fields and weigh two million tons!

swarm—a large group of small animals

Deep oceans

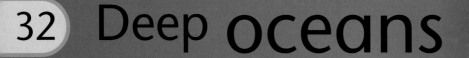

In the deepest parts of the ocean it is always cold and completely dark. The pressure of the water would squash you flat—yet even here there is life.

Deepest divers

Sperm whales dive 1,000 to 10,000 feet down to feed on giant squid. They can hold their breath for almost one hour!

Silver camouflage

Hatchet fish can stay hidden in deep water because they have shiny skin that matches the gleam of the surface far above.

Shine a light

Some animals make
their own light using
chemicals in their
bodies so they can
find each other in
the dark or scare
away predators.

pressure—the weight of water in the ocean

Ocean mysteries

Humans have only just begun to explore life in the sea. There is so much we do not know about some of the biggest and most beautiful marine animals.

Giant mystery . . .

The ocean sunfish, or mola mola, weighs more than 4,000 pounds and eats plankton, but that is almost all we know about this huge fish.

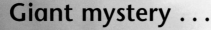

marine animals—*animals that live in or on the sea*

. . . and mysterious giant

Manta rays, or devilfish, can be 20 feet across, but like the sunfish, all we know about them is that they swim through the oceans eating plankton.

Bye-bye, baby!

Baby turtles hatch on sandy beaches and then disappear in the sea. We do not know what they do next, just that they return many years later to breed!

Studying the sea

The ocean is not our home—we cannot breathe underwater, and we are not very good swimmers. However, there are still ways to find out more about the sea.

Follow that seal!
This fur seal has a radio tag attached to its back. It sends signals telling scientists where the seal goes and how deep it dives.

radio tag—*a device that sends out invisible signals that can travel long distances*

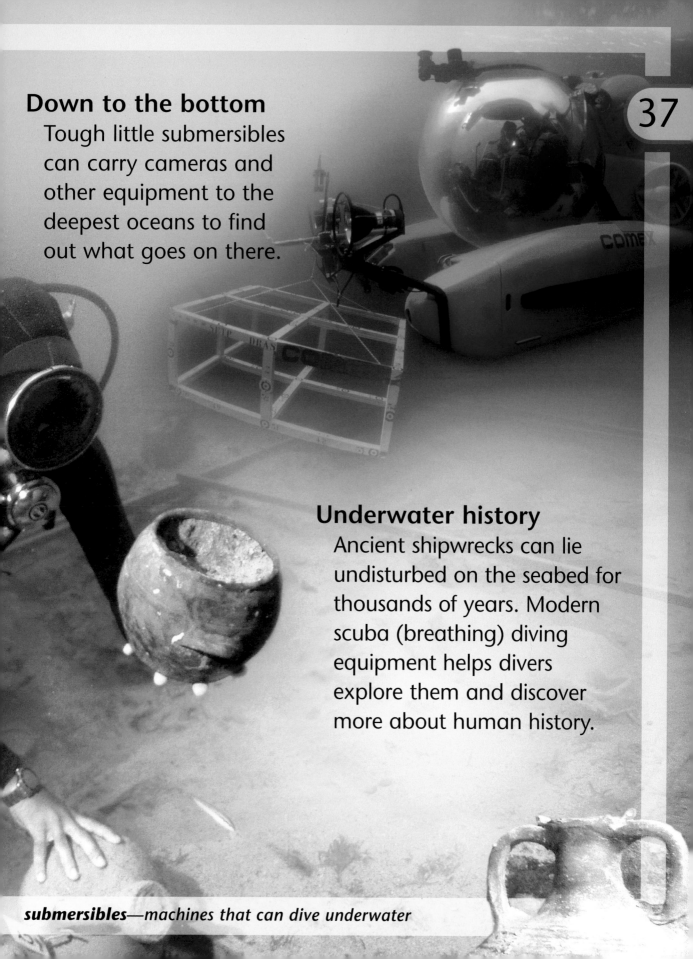

Down to the bottom

Tough little submersibles can carry cameras and other equipment to the deepest oceans to find out what goes on there.

Underwater history

Ancient shipwrecks can lie undisturbed on the seabed for thousands of years. Modern scuba (breathing) diving equipment helps divers explore them and discover more about human history.

submersibles—machines that can dive underwater

All fished out

For thousands of years humans have caught fish to eat. In the past people used simple nets and sailboats. But now we use motorboats and huge nylon nets—the fish do not stand a chance.

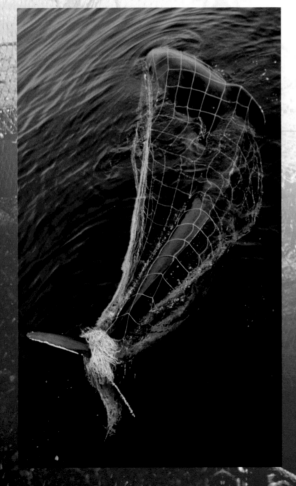

Useless killing

Nets catch anything. Every year millions of dolphins, turtles, sharks, sunfish, and birds die in fishing nets that were supposed to catch something else.

nylon—tough human-made thread

Fishing for trouble

People have become too good at fishing. There are now fewer and fewer fish left to catch. Some fish, such as cod, have almost disappeared!

What a waste!

All over the world people use oceans and seas as garbage cans for all types of trash that kills marine life, but we can stop this from happening.

Stop the spills

If ships carrying oil were made stronger, oil would not spill so easily when the ships crash.

Safe sewage

Sewage can be made safe enough to spread on farmland to help crops grow—not just dumped into the sea.

Perfect plastic

Plastic trash is ugly and can trap and harm marine animals. This waste can be used again or made so that it breaks down naturally.

sewage—body waste that you flush down the toilet

Tasty sea slug

You will need
- Block of marzipan
- Plate
- Food coloring and paintbrush
- Colorful hard candy

A bitter taste
Sea slugs are not eaten by anything in the sea—they taste really horrible! However, here is a sea slug that is tasty to eat.

1

To make the slug's long body, roll the marzipan between your hands into a sausage shape. Then put the shape onto a plate.

2

Many sea slugs have frills. Use your fingers to press down along the bottom edges of the body to make a frill along each side.

3

Dip your paintbrush into some food coloring and paint the frills. The frills can be any color. Paint dots of color down the slug's back.

4

Sea slugs can be very bright. Decorate the slug's body with colorful hard candy. Use two pieces of candy as antennae on the slug's head.

Making waves

Wind power

Wind blowing across the sea makes waves. The stronger the wind, the bigger the waves are. Find out how this happens in this project.

You will need
- Large, clear glass bowl
- Water
- Blue food coloring
- Spoon

Fill the bowl half full with water and add a few drops of blue food coloring. Stir the water to mix.

2 Blow across the surface of the water—this is like wind blowing over the sea. Blow hard, and you will see large waves.

Paper-plate fish

Shiny scales
Fish come in all sizes, shapes, and colors. Use different colors of shiny paper to make a variety of paper-plate fish.

You will need
- Pencil
- Paper plate
- Scissors
- Glue
- Bottle cap
- 1 silver sheet of paper or foil
- 2 colored sheets of shiny paper
- Black marker

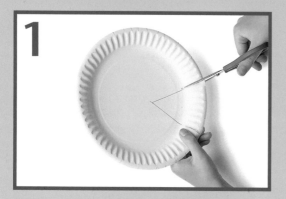

1

Draw a triangle on the plate and cut it out to make a mouth. Glue the triangle piece onto the body, opposite the mouth, to make a tail.

2

Using a pencil, draw around a round bottle cap and make 30 circles on the sheets of shiny paper.

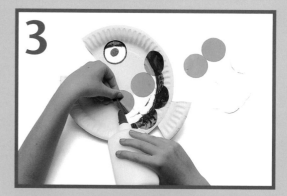

3

Glue on a silver circle above the mouth and draw a black dot in the middle to make the eye. Then stick the other circles onto the body.

Sandy starfish

Many arms—but no legs!
Most starfish have five arms, but some have more than 50! They use their arms to move around and catch prey.

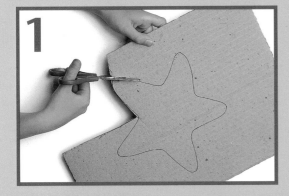

Draw a starfish shape onto the cardboard and cut it out. You can copy the starfish shape from this page.

You will need
- Thick cardboard
- Pencil
- Scissors
- Glue and glue brush
- Teaspoon
- Orange and pink colored sand

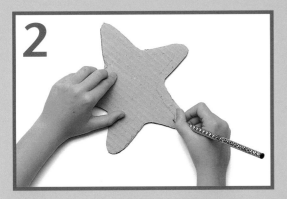

Draw a line that is around one inch from the edge of the starfish, following the starfish shape. Spread glue over the inner starfish shape.

Use the spoon to sprinkle on the orange sand. Press the sand down and leave it to dry. Do the same thing with the pink sand on the edge of the starfish.

Jolly jellyfish

Many tentacles

Jellyfish use their tentacles to gather food as they swim. There are over 200 types of jellyfish, and some have tentacles that are around 30 feet long!

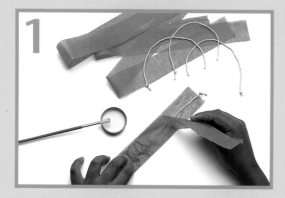

Glue each piece of string down the middle of four strips of tissue paper, from top to middle. Fold up the remaining paper to cover the string.

You will need
- Glue and glue brush
- 4 pieces of string, each 8 in. long
- Green tissue paper cut into 5 strips, each 16 in. long
- Scissors
- Colored paper plate
- Tape
- Shiny paper

Cut the plate in half. Place each green tissue tentacle onto the back of the plate half and stick each one down using tape.

Glue the fifth tissue paper strip along the curve of the plate half. Then cut out circles of shiny paper and decorate the jellyfish body.

Seascape

You will need
- Glue and glue brush
- Green tissue paper, cut into strips
- Large piece of blue poster board
- Sand
- Pen or pencil
- Shiny paper   • Scissors

All together
Here you can create an underwater landscape to show the crafts you have made in this book.

1

Glue the tissue paper strips onto the poster board and spread glue across the bottom. Pour sand over the glue and pat it down.

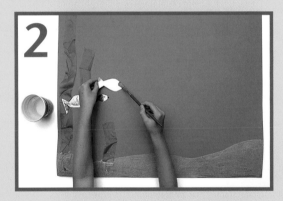

2

Draw fish onto the shiny paper. Cut them out and stick them onto the board. You can also add any other sea animals you have made.

Use different colored tissue paper, shiny paper, and sand to make more sea creatures for your seascape.

Index